ISBN 978-0-243-44008-5
PIBN 10798887

**English**
**Français**
**Deutsche**
**Italiano**
**Español**
**Português**

# www.forgottenbooks.com

**Mythology** Photography **Fiction**
Fishing Christianity **Art** Cooking
Essays Buddhism Freemasonry
Medicine **Biology** Music **Ancient
Egypt** Evolution Carpentry Physics
Dance Geology **Mathematics** Fitness
Shakespeare **Folklore** Yoga Marketing
**Confidence** Immortality Biographies
Poetry **Psychology** Witchcraft
Electronics Chemistry History **Law**
Accounting **Philosophy** Anthropology
Alchemy Drama Quantum Mechanics
Atheism Sexual Health **Ancient History**
**Entrepreneurship** Languages Sport
Paleontology Needlework Islam
**Metaphysics** Investment Archaeology
Parenting Statistics Criminology
**Motivational**

# SHADOWS

## The Creighton University Magazine

VOL. XV, NO. 4                                             JUNE, 1924

## CONTENTS

Published five times during the school year. Subscription: $1.50 per year; single copy, 35c. Entered as second-class matter at the Postoffice at Omaha, Nebraska, under the Act of March 3, 1879. Acceptance for mailing at special rate of postage provided for in section 1103, Act of October 3, 1917, authorized on July 2, 1918. All communications should be addressed to the Shadows, 25th and California Streets, Omaha, Nebraska.

# Graduation

$I$N college days our thoughts were wont to fly
   Within a realm to which enchantment lent
   A touch of glamour to the hours well spent,
A regal splendor tinged with purple dye.

The happiest years of man behind us lie
   When life begins to veer towards serious bent,
   And anxiously we scan with grave intent
The approach of darkening shadows in the sky.

When pleasant thoughts of college days return,
   As oft they will, far vistaed down the years
   Our present vexing cares will seem as dross
Amid the chastened incense that shall burn
   In token of sweet thoughts and sweeter tears
   With which the Senior bore his weighty cross.

—Stephen A. Spitznagle.

# SHADOWS—

## The Creighton University Magazine

,. XV.        JUNE, 1924        No. 4

# )oes a College Degree
# Count in Business

*rviewed by*      *An Old Grad Tells How His College Training*
**Л. R. MECHTENBERG**      *Helped Him to Make a Niche in the Business World*

RIENDS of Creighton are no doubt curious to know what the fates have held in store for the many grads who year after ` assemble on the Hill when the ıelor's degrees are conferred up- he worthy.

To what extent," they may ask ıselves, "does a well-organized ›ge course benefit them in the ld outside—the practical world ısiness?"

ıe answer may be found in the on and the work of T. S. McCaf- , a typical graduate of the college ırts and Sciences. Back in 1907 McCaffrey set forth from the , armed with his Bachelor's de- ›, a goodly supply of common e, and his own innate capacity hard work.

T. S. McCAFFREY,
Graduate of Creighton College of
Arts and Sciences.

found him at his desk, busily engaged in conver- on over the telephone. The spacious new quarters he firm of which Mr. McCaffrey is president give ıle testimony of his achievement in the business ld. I remembered watching the start of this or- ization some few years ago, and marvelled to note progress that so short a time had brought.

oming through the display room I had stopped to ıire a Lincoln touring car and I was still day- ıning over it when Mr. McCaffrey hung up the re- cr and turned to me. Picture him wiry, alert, full

of animation, a man whose outward appearance betrays the keenness characteristic of one who must hold and control the many strings that regulate the multifarious affairs of a large business house.

GETTING through the prelimi- naries as quickly as possible, we plunged immediately into the discussion of the market value of a bachelor's degree. "First of all," Mr. McCaffrey began, "after you have successfully undergone the 'cap and gown' ordeal of Commence- ment Day, you set out to seek a po- sition. And the fact that you pos- sess a college degree does really help to make a good impression. It gives you a prestige among employers that is lacking in the case of the or- dinary applicant. You feel, too, that you have a high ideal to live up to and you realize that your friends and business associates expect you to live up to it. When once you are launched in the business world you find that you must meet and solve problems that are intricate and trying. There it is that you are gratified to see how the rigorous discipline of college training comes to your aid. You realize what before, perhaps, you took on faith, that the disciplined mind is the best tool for doing work. It is not so much the particular facts or theories that you have studied that assist you now, but rather the great fact that you have learned how to use your head.

"I do not want to give the impression, however, that the courses in themselves do not contain valuable material. On the contrary, I believe that nothing is of more practical importance than, for instance, a good training in rhetoric, oratory, expression, and public speaking. This training enables a man to stand up with confidence when it is time to express an opinion before others. And I may remark that the ability to speak clearly and cogently is a great business asset. Too few students seem to appreciate the full value of such societies as your Oratorical Association. Again, I have found that the course in Physics, particularly the principles of mechanics, has helped me directly in my auto and tractor business. Yet the information acquired in a college course is really of secondary importance. Sources of information are always available. But the college trained man knows where to seek the sources and how to use the information."

"WHAT is of greatest aid," continued Mr. McCaffrey, "is the background of general training. In college, stress is laid on principles. A soldier is trained in the fundamentals of military discipline in order that he may be an effective fighter in the time of need; but he should not become an automaton as a result of this training. His training, properly taken, really makes of him a self-reliant, resourceful individual. Now a college training, leading to a bachelor's degree, is as helpful for business life as is the soldier's training in military discipline, for efficiency in the camp or on the battlefield. It is a time-saver. Without it a man is handicapped in his endeavor to climb the ladder of success. He can never substitute for a college course by any experience he may receive in business lines."

"What would you suggest, Mr. McCaffrey, that a non-professional graduate undertake?"

"It does not make a great amount of difference what kind of business he enters, so long as he is careful to choose one in which he feels that he can take a hearty interest with reasonable opportunity for advancement.

If he likes his work and is willing to pursue it z ously, he will succeed."

"Would you mind telling some of your own ex iences, I asked?"

"For about a year and a half after graduation," replied, "I did clerical work, and then took up sa manship, and continued at it till the opportunity entering this business presented itself. Since th that is, during the last six or seven years, I have b kept so busy that I have found little time for anyth else. There isn't much to tell, but I have found ple to keep me occupied.

MANY people are of the impression that no one has any use for a general college education except literary men or those who intend to become instructors. They idealize the "self-made" man and have nothing but unlimited disdain for the so-called "impractical Arts courses."

The successful man himself, however, sees things from a different viewpoint. If he has had the advantage of a college education, there is nothing for which he would exchange his experience. If he has not, he does not hesitate to acknowledge his loss. He realizes that his ignorance of Literature, Philosophy, Science and the other liberalizing studies means an actual loss to him in dollars and cents. More and more he is coming to realize that there is no substitute for a general college training.

"AS for the mere pos sion of a degre concluded Mr. McCaff "it is needless to say tha alone will not ensure succ A capacity for hard work necessary quality in business man who intend get ahead. Without the to do, a degree is usel and the time spent in taining it is wasted."

Such is the business osophy of Mr. McCaff His is a busy, well-ord life, as the message he se indicates. His achievem are due, in a large part a willingness to work, to the advantages which derived from a well-bala course in college.

His example is inspi to the students of Arts Sciences, especially to those who may have entertai some doubts as to the practicability of their train It is the example of a man whose common-sense courage enabled him to make full use of his ad tages—advantages which, when once received, never be taken away, but which, unless a man ap himself with diligence, will not of themselves as him of success. They are merely a means, not an They are the source of those ideals which he will c with him into the world—ideals which will enable to cheerfully accept whatever the future holds, b success or disappointment.

May those seniors who intend to enter comme pursuits find inspiration in Mr. McCaffrey's worl give them the will to do and the energy to succeed

# Enforcement *in*

y J. C.
*ustration by Steve Narkevitz*

# Little River

T ain't worth it!''
The small, red,
wiry man spoke
emphatically, as
token of resignation
h a n d e d "Boss''
wers a glistening
riff's badge, togeth-
with a rather formid-
e Colt, the second
ien of an important
ice.

'Well, ——— ———,
you quittin', too?''
nost moaned Powers.

'Nothin' else, 'Boss'.
ust to be jake gun-
l' for rustlers, but
s here chasin' boot-
gers is dangerous,
d gets all the boys agin' ya.
reckon it's back punchin'
ws on the Bar K for me.''
With this off his mind the
tle fellow ambled to his mount, unteth-
ed it, and rode away.

"Boss'' looked about rather bewilderedly for a mo-
ent from the front stoop of his own establishment,
e Dusty Burro, hotel, restaurant, and bar to Cactus
end. He glanced up and down the only thorough-
re of the town that could be termed a street. Few
gns of activity disturbed the quiet of the warm July
orning. The row of hitching-posts in front of the
ded green facade of the Dusty Burro had just lost
e last rein to be tied there until noon.

THERE were several things to trouble "Boss.'' The
star and gun would not let him forget the vacancy
r sheriff. He expected this, anyway. Two bootleg-
rs of the Idabel settlement had, the evening before,
en indiscreet enough to fire six mischievous shots in
e general direction of the ex-magistrate, when one
ould have sufficed to frighten him out of office. To
ake the affair less seemly, he had ignominiously
ught refuge behind a water trough, without firing

a return shot to uphold the dignity of the law.

AS the leading political figure in the Little River
district of lower Idaho, "Boss'' had long as-
sumed the duty of naming the sheriff.
There were, it is true, biennial elections,
but these were formalities. Moreover,
since election day was two months off,
somebody must meanwhile be appoint-
ed and sanctioned by the eagerly given
approval of docile county commission-
ers. "Boss'' w o u l d
h a v e welcomed a n y
likely candidate.

Although Little Riv-
er County was a flat,
sandy, s u n - c o o k e d
square of the Great
American Desert, it had
become an oasis for
thirsty cowmen. "Boss''
supported heart and
soul the enforcement of
the eighteenth amend-
ment, much as he had
opposed its adoption.
Few of his friends fathomed his changed attitude.
Many were aware that several suspiciously un-
bonded pints had passed over the counter of the Dusty
Burro. No fool was "Boss.'' For a while bootlegging
had been profitable to him; but keen competition stead-
ily lowered the price of the forbidden commodity, until
he now felt that such business was not lucrative enough
to be honorable. In former days Cactus Bend had
been a center of business and pleasure; now the less
worthy towns of Idabel and Cimarron were encroach-
ing on its long enjoyed position of superiority. An
active sheriff would seriously hamper out-county traf-
fic in booze; while the law of supply and demand would,
under the proper conditions, raise the price per unit
volume.

BESIDES the need of a sheriff to be, "Boss'' had
another concern of some uncertainty and impor-
tance. He owned the Double Bar, the best ranch in

the county—although the superlative was hardly flat-
tering. The foreman upon whom had rested the re-
sponsibility of general management was about to
leave. Good foremen were scarce, and "Boss" had
half decided to devote himself to ranching and sell his
interests at the Bend. But the fact that he had a
younger brother in Texas who showed some promise
as a puncher, had changed his mind. "Tex"—for
everybody from the "Lone Star" state must always be
so called—was to arrive this morning on the impro-
vised Ford bus plying between Cactus Bend and the
nearest station. "Boss" put the badge and weapon
into his coat pocket, and sat down on the low porch
edge to wait for his brother.

The punctilious bus soon churned its asthmatic way
up the road, stopping as usual before the Dusty Burro.

"Reckon this is your place," the driver said to
"Tex," the only passenger. "I'll take your stuff into
the hotel."

"Tex" stepped out, a well-built, square shouldered,
bronzed young man, with regular features shaded by a
broad velour sombrero. He wore a pink shirt badly
matching the blue bandana about his neck. He car-
ried no gun, but was girded by a wide, heavily studded
belt supporting corduroy trousers that lost themselves
in a pair of high heeled top boots.

"Boss" was delighted. He had left "Tex" as a boy
of fourteen; ten years had developed and hardened
the younger brother.

"Tex" extended his hand and they greeted one an-
other in the warm, almost rough, western fashion.

"Let's go in so you can get washed and fed before
we talk business, kid," "Boss" suggested, after a short
exchange of news. "Say, by the way, who's sheriff
at Ricardo on the Panhandle now?" he added as an
afterthought.

"Simpkins. I think I'd 'ave got the job, if you
hadn't sent for me."

"You was gonna be sheriff?"

"Yeah," answered "Tex."

"Boss" began to think. He showed "Tex" into the
Dusty Burro. Inside the door a cigar counter also
served as a desk for guests to register. On the same
side a long bar, scarred by indelicate cowboys, stretched
to the back of the place. The rest of the room, form-
erly used for dancing, was broken here and there by
tables at which a young lady was busy placing paper
napkins.

As the two came in she turned around.

"This," smiled "Boss," "is Peggy. She lives with
her folks in town, and is in full charge of the Burro
from nine to four."

H E would have liked to add that Peggy was the
only object of which the Bend was really proud,
and that "Tex" need not be surprised to have her for

# SONGS *in a* Shower Room

### By PAUL FITZGIBBON

*Illustration by Darrell Downs*

IT is a favorite superstition of the popular mind that wine and song are the two inseparables, the indispensables of joy and mirth. But it is only a superstition foisted upon us by the race of poets. s a matter of fact there is no necessary relation of ause and effect between the sip of nectar and the igbt of song. Plain humble water will do as much to ispire a lusty tenor as the choicest Port.

This assertion will, no doubt, be challenged as the inkest heresy. Have not the bards from Homer to my Lowell extolled the virtues of the vine, the preirsor and companion of melody? Not even Gil Blas, r all his respect for "the universal dissolvent", would ave the temerity to question red wine as the prime over of song. Such boldness invites insult.

Well, then, let the poet betake himself to the shower-oom of a gymnasium. There he will hear a basso-pro-indo struggling with "Asleep in the Deep", and an bortive tenor strangling on "Dear Old Pal of Mine". aritones are yodelling, and those with no voice at all re trying the intricate intervals of "The One I Love." fo drinking bout ever described in poetry or fiction ould possibly be more fruitful of bad music. If the oet's analytical turn require him to seek the reason,

likely he will not find it. The symptoms are evident enough, but the disease is more obscure.

It may be that men feel freest at their cleansing. Perhaps it is the magic of the shower-room that gives mere water such an exhilirating effect. But leave it to the philosopher to explain the why and wherefore. It is the business of the poet to catch the spirit of the life he would put into song. Then, let him divest himself and join in the ablutions. He will soon cease to wonder and begin to sing.

Nor will anyone dispute his right. It makes no difference how badly he sings. No one will appear to notice it, much less to censor him for it. If he sings weakly, his neighbor will join and help him. If he demonstrates a considerable gusto, his neighbor will yell the louder. There is nowhere such goodwill and tolerance of vocal effort as in the shower-room. I know that I have sung there without restriction in the hearing of men whom neither bribery nor intrigue would bring to hear me in any other circumstance.

Our inquiring poet will find that some songs are better adapted to shower-rooms. When Caruso sang the beautiful Neapolitan love song, "O Sole Mio," it was

(Continued on Page 37).

**P**ROFESSOR HENRY A. PERKINS of Trinity College has entered a very vigorous protest against the importance that present educational practice places upon extra-curricular activity. In "The American College," an article in "The North American Review" for April, he makes the point that scholarship is suffering because the average student devotes an excessive amount of time to athletics, forensics,

# *The* Creightor

*By* THE PRESIDEN

REV. M. J. GORMAN,
Author of The Passion Play as presented by
the Creighton Dramatic Club.

dramatics and other forms of activity which are not a part of the regular courses. It is his contention that the tendency to concentrate student attention on activities which lie outside the curriculum is working harm to the real interests of the American college.

This protest of Professor Perkins is representative of a fairly general feeling among leaders of educa-

tional thought that too much energy is being direc outside the curriculum. There can be no doubt t this tendency actually exists in the American colle Accordingly, Professor Perkins' contention seems be very much in order.

**T**O what degree this tendency is seen in the fi of dramatics varies, of course, in different insti tions. There is little doubt, however, that the coll dramatic club is generally a grievous sinner in the m ter of taking the student's time away from stud The successful production of a play involves so mu work on the part of the participants that other int ests must inevitably suffer. It is pretty well rec nized by both teachers and students that school w is likely to suffer during the preparation of a play. seems, then, that Professor Perkins has some basis complaint in his protest against the college dram club.

But no such complaint can properly be ente against dramatics at Crei ton. It is generally conce that we have too little r er than too much dram activity here. Far from err on the side of excess, Crei ton dramatics have had har enough prominence to attr their fair amount of student tention. Only a very limi number of students have gi any time to dramatic work, they have been supported b disappointingly small por of the student body. If c maties have any right at al college life, it must be admit that they have not reac their proper place at Creight and that a policy which p poses more dramatics is wo consideration.

CRUCIFIXION SCENE FROM THE PASSION PLAY.

# )ramatic Club

ᐊHAT dramatics should occupy a properplace in college life is agreed by everyone. It is not necessary :esort to the new psychology to prove the cultural ue of dramatic expression. That is a matter of ımon experience. Anyone who has taken part in a y will recognize that the experience has helped him ›ome way or other. It may have given him an ease confidence in public that he might otherwise have ked. It may have helped him to acquire the polish l suavity of the characters he acted. Certainly it developed his powers of observation and mimicry. ; mere "going through the motions" of a crisis in ther's life is bound to be a factor in one's own emoıal development. It is fairly obvious that dramatic ›erience rightly forms a very real part of a college n's training.

n addition to its strictly cultural value, dramatic ivity satisfies a kind of instinctive craving of the nan spirit. The fascination of the footlights holds ally for the tried actor and the uninitiated amar. Everyone at some time in his life has an ambiı to take part in a play, even though it be but to tray the humble part of policeman or lackey. To able to disguise oneself with grease-paint and false r is to become part of a great tradition. He has sed one of the greatest ills of life who has never ered before an audience h fateful words as, "Is Juhere?" or "I love her! I e her!" There can be no bt that participation in dra:ics, when held within prop-.imits, furnishes the student h an experience that is at e profitable and pleasurable.

ᐊHE present Creighton Dramatic Club represents an empt to fill the need for dra:ic activity in the Univer-'. It represents the beging of a policy which promises to dramatics at Creighton a position which is consistent with their importance in student life. The Club was organized only last October. The membership was kept small and selected, only those who had taken part in previous University plays being eligible to join. This was done designedly in order that the newly formed club might function successfully from the start. A large organization in the beginning might be unwieldy,

CHARLES S. COSTELLO,
Professor of Expression and Director of the
C. U. Dramatic Club.

and consequently lose the advantage of centralized effort. The policy adopted was vindicated by the success met in "Turn to the Right" and "Innovations." Members of the club took important roles in the Passion Play and aided materially in making this presentation the high mark in Omaha amateur dramatic productions. All who have been interested, agree that the club has done splendid work in its first year.

But a limited membership and a more or less re-

(Continued on Page 31)

SCENE FROM "TURN TO THE RIGHT".

# *To the Flag*

Flag of a glorious nation, hail!
We greet thee and proclaim anew the ties
That hold thee ever dear.
A nation in the balance lay,
Oppression stared on every side.
Then Freedom in her anguish cried,
And thou wert born.

The bitter snows of Valley Forge
Thy white supplied—thy red,
The countless thousands who have died,
That thou mightst live.
Thy blue from heaven's breast was torn,
By eagles to thy staff was borne—and lo!
The gleaming stars adhered.

At Concord Bridge was thy spirit felt,
At Gettysburg in silence knelt a nation
While thy fate was weighed.
O'er Argonne's Wood where shrapnel screamed
High midst the clouds thy figure gleamed;
And they below, could they refuse
That silent plea?

What though 'twas death that lurked before,
What though the foe in ambush lay,
What though the tortured, riven earth
Shrank from the deadly cannonade,
With eyes upon thy starry field,
With hearts whose strength would never yield—
    thou called—
They carried-on.

They carried-on, and lightly held the cost,
The heart-ache and the thousand severed ties,
The grief—they followed and thou ledst the w
To fields of honor through the paths of death.
They died—but thou above triumphant fly.
O God that we could learn to live
As they have learned to die.

Flag through a thousand perils borne,
Oft stained with blood with shrapnel torn,
True guardian of the sacred trust
In thee reposed,
Far from the War God's withering breath,
Thou callest to a nobler day.
We follow through life as they through death,
Lead thou the way.

ADDISON V. BRANDON.

# Nice Little Puppy

*Illustration by Darrell Downs*

*By* EMMET M. GREEN

THE room had that peculiar, musty odor that is associated with a poorly ventilated human habitation. Its tall, stark furniture, grotesquely silhouetted against the misty silver light of early ɪorn, might have put one in mind of a group of solemn ʍls gazing out from the silence of their dark reʈeat. The illusion was suddenly shattered by a beam ʄ light that began to play erratically over the walls.

A humped shadow slipped into the room. There was soft swish · of rug under foot. His method of apʈoach proved the intruder to be a novice at the game. ɪe kept his light too much in evidence; he hesitated ʈhen the time for hesitation was past. This was a ew experience for Abie Finkelstein, and one that ɪvored too much of the adventurous to suit his peaceʌl disposition. Abie was a good natured, well-roundɪl, and moderately industrious young Israelite, with a ʌspicion of a mustache, a slightly bald spot, and an ppetite for late suppers and chorus girls. A close ealer with men, he had been known to do a startling ʙout-face when skillfully handled by one of the oppoʈe sex.

Abie's courage was on the wane. His whole body ʌas atremble. He snapped out the light and stood ith one moist hand clamped on the corner of the ʙrary table, trying to recall his fleeting spirit.

ROBBERY, especially of one's father, is a ticklish business, and no one was more thoroughly conʈious of the fact than Abie himself. His breath came ʌspingly through his throat and he considered what ɪs position would be, should his stern and bewhiskered ʈre suddenly stand before him. At the thought, he ɪvoluntarily stepped back, and even raised his free ɪand to his face as if to ward off a blow. Then the ʈcurring thought of Lollie subdued his fear. Lollie ɪaRue was a cabaret dancer, and a young lady of some ʌash, but of most uncertain temper, a failing which she ɪplained was a debt all artists must pay to their art. ɪow could Abie face her without the money? He must ʈhe must go through with it.

Taking firm hold of himself, he tried to go briskly ʙout the business; so briskly, in fact, that his hand ɪ leaving the table carried the phone with it. He alɪʘst screamed in terror at the sharp report of its fall.

He was now one mass of shiver interspersed regularly with giant quakes that almost robbed him of the power to stand. He listened intently for signs of movement in the house, but could hear only the blood pounding in his ears. Cold perspiration rolled down his sleek sides. Gradually remnants of his courage returned, and he set about the task of drilling into the lock, desperately and awkwardly. He trembled so · violently that he could scarcely keep the drill in place, but he labored feverishly, and, as all things must come to an end, his work at length neared completion.

He was nervously trying to ignite the fuse, when, with a blinding flash, the lights of the library suddenly snapped on, followed instantly by the savage bark of a pistol. Abie spun around on his heel, his eyes starting, his hand clutched over his heart. He had but time to catch a fleeting glimpse of the ghost-like apparition of his father, in white night-shirt and with smoking gun, when he fell heavily to the floor.

Mr. Finkelstein senior, despite his years, displayed considerable agility. Hurriedly he snatched up the 'phone and frantically jangled the receiver-hook. Operators are notoriously hard to arouse during these hours.

Hello—HELLO! Where are you?—Op'rator! Come kvick on the 'phone——HELLO!——Where in——Oh, mein Got!"

Mr. Finkelstein was getting into a tremendous sweat.

"Hello! Answer! Answer—for just once!"

It was a wail of despair.

"Hello, central!"—He heard a wee, petulant voice. ——I vant you should connect me to the police—No— police—POLICE—P-O-L-I-S-E—police."

He waited a moment, nervously tapping his fingers on the table and stealing fearful glances at the prostrate and motionless form on the floor. He thought he heard a click in the receiver.

"Hello! Is this you, the police? Hello! I want you should send some police to my place—kvick—to my place—here—I am Finkelstein—the seeds man—hurry —There is murder and a robbery!"

Wiping the perspiration from his face as he kept one eye on the prostrate intruder, Mr. Finkelstein tremblingly replaced the receiver. What to do!

Should he go to the assistance of the fallen man? It seemed inhumanly cruel to allow him to welter there until the police arrived. True, the man had sought to rob him, to steal from him the very prop that sustained his house. Yet he was a fellow human, who, even at that moment, might be in frightful pain. Where had he been wounded? The old man could see no evidences of blood; but then, very little light shone where the man lay. Finkelstein looked around the room, nervously. Suppose the man had an accomplice, who even now might be stealing upon him unawares. But no; that did not seem likely, else he certainly would have come in before; if indeed the noise of the shooting had not frightened him away. Finkelstein thought something of awakening his wife, when, on turning to his former position, he noticed to his infinite terror, that the man was begin-

ning to stir. This was a contingency that Mr. Finkelstein had not looked for. Now indeed, his situation was serious. Suppose the man should rise up and shoot him! Horrible thought. If Finkelstein was frightened before, he was terror-stricken now. Clutching his pistol, he strained his eyes to pierce the darkness of the farther room. Subconsciously he was aware of the first grey tints of dawn but

YOU ARE A BUMMER. NOTHING BUT A BUMMER

one thing he did not notice was that a loose thread of the fuse continued to smolder with the very faintest of glows. Slowly the man on the floor raised one hand, then dropped it, sighed, and rolled partly over.

Mr. Finkelstein stiffened and rose to his feet. He held his gun out an arm's length and waved it in the general direction of the enemy. His other arm he stretched out to the rear as if to hold open the way of possible retreat. In this ghoulish attitude, with his white night shirt gently playing about his withered frame, he stole slowly and silently toward the intruder.

THE man stirred again, and muttered something and Finkelstein, startled, paused for a moment. Then, looking fearfully about the room, he took a few more steps. He was now almost directly over the man, and had he examined him closely, must certainly have recognized him. But Finkelstein senior was not in the least curious about the identity of his prisoner. His

attention was entirely taken up with his own saf Despite his trepidation, he was firmly resolved that burglar should not have another opportunity to him of his treasure. Between his natural fears fo personal safety and his inherited solicitude for money, he was in a truly pitiable plight. Neverthe he resolved to stand his ground.

Abie, at the time of the shooting, was working very high pitch of excitement. A very slight jolt w suffice to throw his nerves off center. Therefore, the lights had flashed up so startingly, only to be lowed by that crashing pistol report, Abie had i ined himself hit, and in this thought had lost comr of his faculties. Now he was coming to, and, as if f the effects of a bad dream, he was experiencing siderable difficulty in finding his bearings. He lay a long moment ga dully through t parted eyelids. was vaguely awar white-clad fi g pointing a bright ject at his head. S denly his eyes wid and he raised him on his elbow. gesture was met the strangely ster somewhat quave voice of the e "Down! Don't moof, you low-l if you want me to day-light in you.' he said this, Fi stein brandished gun in the other's face.

Abie's fears came back to him with a rush, " you don't know it? Its me!''

The hand that wielded the gun suddenly cam rest. "What you tell me? Stop?" He leaned fa down. It's not you—'' His voice broke. "I couldn't be my—''

The sentence we must suffer to remain unfini With a terrific roar the safe burst open, parts o wall fell down, and Abie, accompanied this time b disilllusioned parent, departed again for that pea land from which he had so lately returned.

The dust settled and all was quiet. But not for A distant rumble, as if from thunder, came from al Apparently the explosion had been a disturban sufficient proportions to awaken Mrs. Finkelstein presently, with tremendous exertion, she came lun ing down-stairs, in such a manner, indeed, that it se

(Continued on Page 29)

# ⌐wo Views of CONRAD

## By THE KONRAD KULT

IKE so many other first impressions, my first impression of Joseph Conrad was distinctly unfavorable and unfair. "Too much description"
was the superficial indictment with which I
nissed him, after what I must confess was anything
a fair trial. My first sample of Conrad's magic
e was "The Nigger of the Narcissus," which I
g aside in disgust before I had fairly started it.
plot there was little that could be detected with
naked eye; and action was conspicuous only for its
city. The book was, in
uncritical opinion, just a
es of rich, cloying deptions.
: is several years since I
. set sail on the seas of
rad, and to this day I
remember just two things
at "The Nigger of the
cissus." One is the imof the magnificent negro
e stepped on deck for the
time; the other, my unuised dislike for both the
ro and the book. Preje may or may not exn my aversion for the
ro; it certainly explains my repugnance for the
k. At this particular age I was a confirmed deption-skipper. As soon as I scented a scrap of
cription, I blithely passed it by without so much as
od of recognition. I eschewed description as thorhly as the Barefoot Boy ever eschewed his books
tasks. It was following the line of least resistance,
naps, but such a course is not altogether indefens
. What difference does it make to me whether
nhoe's sandals were laced with a buckskin cord,
with an anachronistic shoestring manufactured at
l River, Massachusetts? I do not mean to imply
t Conrad belongs to the Scott school of description,
se tedious triviality and minuteness has long since
n discarded as chaff. But at the time that I read the
igger of the Narcissus" all description looked alike
ne. It was something to be avoided, and not visued, disdained and not recreated. Being therefore

such an implacable foe to description, it was only
natural that I should dislike Conrad, whose forte is
description.

Open hostilities between Conrad and myself were
suspended for the time being. But last summer an
event occurred which brought me out of my state of
passive hostility. It was the pilgrimage which Conrad, like all orthodox English writers, paid to the
United States. His visit created a considerable stir in
literary circles. He was hailed as the standard-bearer
of contemporary fiction;
deafening huzzas assailed his
ears everywhere; and every
magazine with literary aspirations or pretensions
joined in the universal
chorus of adulation. Amid
all this fawning and salaaming, Conrad became the fad
of the hour, and Conrad cults
sprang up like mushrooms.

It was this literary sensation which was chiefly instrumental in overcoming
my long-standing antipathy
to Conrad. "There must be
something in him after all,"
I reasoned. "Otherwise people wouldn't be making
such a fuss about him." Not until lately, however,
did I silence my forebodings sufficiently to essay a second Conrad novel. With no little trepidation, I commenced to read "The Rescue." I had not read twenty
pages when my trepidation disappeared; twenty pages
more, and I became broadly tolerant of Conrad; another twenty, and I began to reverse my previous verdict; and so on, until finally I became positively enamored of the great English Pole.

THE Rescue is not a great novel in any accepted
sense, but those who have dipped deeply into Conrad agree that it is far from being his best. In spots, interest flags perceptibly; the story seems to be inflated
beyond its natural limits; and the plot is loosely and
wretchedly constructed. In a lesser author, such a
makeshift plot would mean certain oblivion; but since

> "CONRAD'S language seems
> to ebb and flow as regularly
> as the tides which his descriptive
> pen so loves to linger over. The
> writer has succeeded in translat
> ing the unearthly rhythm of the
> sea and the waves into words,
> and with the accuracy of a faith
> ful translator, adapts sound and
> word to mood and action."

(Continued on Page 35)

# "It Might Have Been"

*By* FRANCIS R. BYRNE
*Decoration by Joseph M. Dallal*

$\mathcal{A}$ Comedy *in Three* ~

### CAST OF CHARACTERS

Arthur Morrison - - - - - - A young architect
Irene Morrison - - - - - - - - - - His wife
George Hemingway - - - - - A young bank teller
Ellen Hemingway - - - - - - - - His wife
A policeman

## ACT ONE

Scene—Apartment of the Morrisons. The living room is the replica of thousands of others in three-room apartments throughout this middle-western metropolis, and a description of it would be a waste of words. The telephone bell rings and Irene Morrison enters from the left, sits down and takes up the receiver. She is a good-looking, well-dressed woman of about thirty.

Ir—Yes?—Who?—Oh, Mrs. Gordon, I was just thinking about you. Do you know I had almost made up my mind to call you when the phone rang. What?— Who did?——Well! You don't say! —— I knew there was something wrong; she couldn't fool me, but I never thought it was that bad. ——No, of course not. I'll never tell a soul. —— Of course I won't tell Arthur. You know, they say a woman can't keep a secret; but at that I don't think we're nearly as bad as our husbands. Do you know, Arthur can never keep a thing from me. I scent it a mile off, and I don't rest until I pry it out of him. —— What's that? —— Beg pardon, I didn't get the name. —— Mrs. Norgren! —— Why, do you know, I told her the day before yesterday, and she swore she'd never tell a soul. There's a gossiping woman for you. —— Yes——When?—— Impossible! Why, I saw her at the theatre only this afternoon. —— Oh, I'm so sorry. Must you really go? I had so much to say to you. Well, good-bye. Call me up to-morrow. ——Good-bye. (Hangs up receiver and goes to the table, where she picks up one of the latest illustrated magazines and sits down to read. Her husband comes in, hangs his hat on the rack in the hall, and enters the room.)

Art—Hello, Irene.

Ir—(Lazily) Hello, Arthur.

Art—How's the little wifey tonight? Did you enjoy yourself today?

Ir—No. The matinee was horrid today; one of dull problem plays. You know I like some thrilling, where the hero is a big, handsome You know, where the heroine simply can't him.

Art—Yes, I know what you like. That's all once in a while; but I should think you' tired of that stuff. Some of it is really scand

Ir—Speaking of scandal, Mrs. Gordon was tellin this afternoon about the McKelvys. They l row and now Mrs. McKelvy is going to sue divorce. Mrs. Gordon is the only one who l about it.

Art—She won't be the only one for very long.

Ir—She lives next door and she got the whole I promised I wouldn't tell anyone; so don' go telling it around. (Arthur laughs). Wh you laughing about?

Art—Oh, nothing. Say, do you know the firm contract for a new bunch of houses out on Grove Drive. I am to design some of them I think that perhaps if I make good I'll be i for a promotion.

Ir—Of course I'm glad for your sake, Arthur; bu know I can't get interested in these busine fairs.

Art—Did you see that row of small cottages th Colm Company is building on Riverside vard, near the golf links? They are certainl looking and homelike. When they get trees ed and grass growing it will be a wonderful

Ir—(Dividing her attention between her husban the magazine which she has been holding lap during the conversation). Yes, I saw th

Art—Do you know, I don't care about designing buildings and factories. They are just the day grind to me. But when it comes to desi homes, there is a feeling that holds me and me feel that I am doing something really while. You know there's a sort of roman building houses and imagining what sort of people are going to live in them. Perhaps in the very house which I planned today will be born a man who will rise to fame and honor. It makes one feel more intimate with people, the knowledge of what we have in common.

Really, Arthur, you should have taken up law or politics. Your powers of oratory are marvelous.

—Of course I know you don't see it as I do, but if you were doing the work I am doing, day after day, you'd be enthused, too.

Yes, that's all right, but why don't you try for something better? You know you could have had the work for that new insurance building if you really wanted it. Some big building down town is a great deal better than a lot of little cottages. Whoever asks who drew the plans for this or that house? But the architect for every office building has all kinds of advertising.

—Oh, Irene, can't you understand? That is why I am trying to get away from, this commercializing of the whole business. It's nothing but mechanical work, and it seems so empty.

Still, when you are building factories or office buildings you are aiding the commercial and industrial life of the nation. I should think that it would seem just as ideal to you to be associated with the big enterprises as to be helping to build small houses. And besides, think of having your name in the papers as the architect for some new skyscraper. There's a lot more money in it, too.

—Yes, there is something to the money side of it, and anything that would help us financially shouldn't be sneezed at; but even that sort of work is not steady, and I cannot do as well at it, for I can't put my heart into it. On the other hand there is always a demand for houses, as the town is growing, and I may be able to make a reputation for myself in that line.

Of course I realize and sympathize with your ambitions; but still you are an unpractical idealist.

Art—No, I'm not unpractical; but I'll admit I am an idealist—and my ideal is the home, not merely a house. You know some of these big mansions were not made to live in. They are all right for holding receptions or givng house parties; but they seem so cold and impersonal, not at all the kind of place in which I'd choose to live. And then, on the other hand, these apartments! Take this one for instance. It's just like thousands of others—standardized; not a bit of individuality in it. You come here to sleep or to eat. Just a place to hang your hat. There is no privacy or seclusion; the walls are so thin that you can hear every word the neighbors say. Oh, I am sick and tired of it!

Ir—But you know this is the best we can afford now. A suite at the Colonial would be too expensive for us.

Art—Yes, I know this is the best apartment we can afford; but we could have a home in the suburbs; Forest Lawn, for instance. There's the swellest little six-room cottage there, just finished. If we economized we could own it ourselves. They want only two thousand cash, and we could pay the rest in two years for less than the rent on this place. You know you still have that two thousand your uncle left you.

Ir—Yes, I know. But I don't think we should invest in real estate. What if the prices should go down? And then think of living away out where one would have to ride three quarters of an hour in a stuffy, smelly street car. I like this place here; it's so close to everything. And then think of the work! I know I'd die if I had to do all the housework. Here we have the janitor, and the maid cleans up twice a week. That reminds me, you must report to the company that we are not getting good service from the janitor. I believe he sleeps all day.

Art—All right, I'll remember it; but I can't get that other thing off my mind. It haunts me night and

(Continued on Page 27)

# Vacation

**W**HAT are you going to do this summer? This will be the hardest question to answer in the June semester examinations. If you don't believe me, try to answer it to your own satisfaction in an hour or two, and I assure you that after you read your response you will agree with me that you deserve a zero on that question.

"When are you going home, George?"

"Well, my last exam is from one to three, Friday, and I guess I will take the 3:45 and get home before Sunday." Friday follows Thursday's busy day of packing, and as you shake hands and say good-bye to your pals you receive their hearty wishes for a pleasant summer vacation, and you inevitably return the compliment. But do you really know how you are going to spend that vacation? Have you any plans for a healthful and enjoyable leave from your books? I venture to say that 95 per cent of the Creighton students go home and forget about themselves and through want of foresight waste their vacation. What is a vacation for? Is it the period during which you are allowed to go home and display yourself to the natives, or is it the three months' hard labor term? Will you go home and be the vogue type, comparable to the Farnam street dude? Be the boy with the big head (far too large, by the way, for all that is in it, and with rooms to let); have it surmounted by a very large hat; trousers into which your legs seem to have been melted and poured; a pair of toothpick shoes; an abbreviated topcoat; an eye-glass in your "ocular," and a stick in your hand so thick as to make your legs look thin by comparison; carry your arms at an angle of forty five degrees, and walk like a consumptive kangaroo. Be the creature that makes an old Nebraska farmer exclaim, "Gosh! what things a man do see when he ain't got his gun handy!" Strut the village street and rot with laziness. Or will you go home and toil from morn till night behind the plow or counter, harden your hands with honest work, and forget that you are having a vacation? If you are coming back to school in the fall after spending that first kind of a summer, remember that you haven't had a vacation. Why? Because you didn't know how to take one.

I have spent a great many vacations in varied ways, but all were along healthful lines. In the Christmas

THE WRITER SEATED ON THE RIM OF THE GRAND CANYON.

"Shadows," in conjunction with my pal, I chronicle the events of a long western trip made last summer. That was the most extensive vacation I have ever had. It might be worth while to mention that I do not advise a trip of this kind, since I realize that the financial river of the average Creighton student is as dry at the close of the school year as the washes on the New Mexico deserts. Then, too, assure yourselves that a trip of that kind is filled with many obstacles, and that it takes plenty of pluck to overcome them. I submit a few pictures of my western sojourn at this time merely to show you the barriers I had to overcome in order to gain the Shady Palm prize. The mountains and deserts are far too hard and risky to cross with cheap second-hand equipment. Therefore it is that I advise the average student not to attempt so extensive a trip.

**D**ETOUR with me from your usual way of spending your summer vacation, and I will tell you how and why you should spend the next three months along a healthful path. Some years ago I read a lecture on "Life and Living," by Rev. William Lloyd, and it so impressed me that I immediately had a new outlook on life. With sincere thanks and apologies to the author I will preface his wise thoughts and words for you, since they are really gems. I take the liberty to assume that every young man who reads this article is able to reason. If he reasons he will do as say, and so doing he will have his first real vacation.

The person in this life with a healthy constitution and an education has a grand endowment. That person is the heir to a kingdom. That kingdom is physical life and the universe of light and beauty and order which the Creator has ordered and enriched, that may minister to his pleasure and development. Almost infinite possibilities of enjoyment lie within and before

# Detour

*...ut in enjoying health.---MARTIAL*

### By HAROLD J. BONSTETTER

...at being. His body is endowed with sensations and ...petites and powers, all of which, lawfully used, can ...ing to him great, almost exhaustless delight. Along ...e nerves of sensation run rivers of pleasure. The ...dy is a harp of a thousand strings, and rightly swept ...ey will send forth rich, entrancing melodies. Life ...a song or a wail, as the body is in tune or otherwise. ...is wonderful to have senses and organs through ...hich the light and beauty, the sweetness and har-...ony of such a universe this in which we live ...ay be received and rev-...ed in; by which we can ...ok out upon the beauty ...the landscape, to be-...ld its wondrous changes ...light and shadow; gaze ...on the sunlight and the ...ars; hear the music of ...thousand voices, the ...ng of birds, the chant ...the winds playing with ...seen hands upon trees, ...e solemn music of the ...ver-marching waves, wakening thrills of speechless ...ladness in the soul; inhale the perfume of the flowers ...ast lavishly upon every passing breeze; and above all ...ese realize the charm of sweet, pure friendship, the ...apture of love, the joys of home.

THE world is full of beauty—beauty enough to minister to the artistic taste of every human be-...ng. You don't have to travel a thousand miles to ...ee it, nor do you have to vision it with your imagina-...on. There is enough good scenery within a hundred ...iles from where you are to crown with beneficent ...lessings every human soul on the face of the earth. I ...ave no sympathy with the spirit which will not see ...nd feel and be thrilled by the loveliness of the world ...a which we live. I get out of patience with the miser-...ble religious sentimentalism that is so taken up with ...reams of heaven as to have no eye to see and no heart ...o respond to the beauty there is in this life. When I ...ear people slandering their lot and this grand old ...arth as a howling wilderness or a dead hole, I feel like

saying, "Well, you certainly do your share of the howling or killing." I must confess to a passionate love of the beautiful in the world I live in, and a thrill of intense pleasure sometimes, in the very fact of exist-ence. There have been days in my life so full, so rap-turous that I cared not whether there came a tomor-row. Have you ever stood, as I have, upon a mountain summit, with a broad, calm lake lying at your feet, a valley stretching away yonder dotted with villages, on whose church steeples the sunlight flashed its first greeting in the morning, and lingered at even-tide for a last good night; while, far away, peak after peak of snow-clad mountains lifted themselves up into the heavens of a cloudless sky? Have you ever gazed at night into the sky, thick with stars, glorious with the moon walking in her brightness? Have you ever stood by the ocean and let the breeze, wet with brine, fan your brow, and watched the breakers curling and tum-bling in upon the shore, whose snowy crests the poet

A TYPICAL CALIFORNIA ORANGE ORCHARD.

likens to the white fleeces of flocks that are never folded? Have you listened to the song of the birds on a summer morn, or the passionate trills of the nightingale "sweet sing-ing to his mate?" Have you looked into the faces of little children, seen the joy and delight that they experience in simply liv-ing and breathing? beheld the love light in their eyes, heard the merry ring of their laughing voices? Have you felt the thrill of a glance from eyes that from the fringed lids spoke what the lips dared not utter? Have you realized that with a healthy body and a clean moral nature, in the midst of this universe you are an instrument finely at-tuned, on which all the thousand fingers of nature do play, every nerve a chord, every emotion a tone, every sense thrilling with ecstacy? Have you? Then you have in every sense entered into the Kingdom of Life.

NOW if you want to trot out into the pasture of a healthy and happy vacation you must enter in at the gate. That gate is obedience to the laws of your physical and moral nature. These laws are woven into the very warp and woof of your being. This universe is a universe of law. The heavens above tell it in their starry speech, and the hands of the frost write it in beautiful crystaline forms on the window panes.

Everywhere order, through telescope or microscope or spectroscope. Through whatever instrumentality,

(Continued on Page 27)

Shadows Staff.

# Retrospect

W ITH this, the final issue of SHADOWS, the staff extends its heartfelt thanks to all those who, by their active support and encouragement, have helped to make the year a success. In particular it has been gratifying to observe the willingness shown by members of the various departments to contribute their time and work in the hope of doing something for SHADOWS and for the school it represents. Our only wish is that this same willingness to serve will be augmented as the years go on.

The aim of every university magazine in providing a medium of expression for the student body as a whole, is to reflect the spirit and life of the institution of which it is a part. But the life of a university is varied. It is a mixture of work and play; the serious is blended with the whimsical. It has been our purpose to catch and reflect the phases of this life with its varying lights and shadows. To this end we have combined the serious with the humorous, the satirical with the grave, always bearing in mind that the vast majority of the readers are students.

The ultimate goal of our achievement is a magazine that combines the highest degree of literary merit compatible with material which is both entertaining and profitable. Obviously, such an ideal can not be realized over night. It will be, perhaps, several years before SHADOWS will occupy the throne intended for it. In the meantime, the success or failure of each successive staff will be measured by the distance they have advanced toward this goal.

# For the Coming Year

I N order to keep alive the keen interest manifested by the student body in their magazine, and to assure a continuation of the freshness and verve necessary to such a vital force in college life, the custom of appointing a new managing editor at the close of each year has been established. In accordance with this policy, the staff has chosen Addison V. Brandon to fill that office during the ensuing year. Under his guidance, with the co-operation of all departments, SHADOWS cannot fail to improve and go forward.

Contributions to the Poets' Corner will always be welcomed by the Poetry Editor. The Shadows' Sanctum is room 269 in the College of Arts.

We aim to make this column representative of the University rather than of a few writers. May we list you among our contributors?

## COLUMBIA
### By R. A. J.

All hail to thee, thou sacred shrine,
Thou hallowed land of heroes true,
Thou staunchest rock in stormy times,
Thou sturdy bark of liberty.
A helping, saving hand art thou,
A welcome refuge from oppression.
All hail to thee, thou ocean gem,
O'ershadowed by the stars and stripes!
Protect us from a tyrant's greed,
A heartless monarch's iron hand;
Let ne'er a sceptre's shadow chill
The fervor of thy children's love.

## SERENADE
### By EPIMETHEUS

The first pink buds of blooming Dawn
Are tinting now the eastern sky;
The mist hangs low o'er field and lawn;
Awake, my Love, and let us fly.

Unseen, the first lark sings above
That he will e'er be true.
The first lark sings to his lady-love
And I—I sing to you.

Awake, we've all the night for grief.
Life's morn is ours, oh, be not shy:
The night is long, but morn—how brief—
Awake, my Love, awake, 'tis I.

A bewitching moon, a star-kissed lake,
And thee at right hand oar,
Then all would bend to sweet romance,
And love forevermore.

Full many a heart with quickened beat
Has on a lake been caught,
For easiest the net enwraps
The heart by moonlight sought.

## INSPIRATION
### By S. A. S.

The shadowy wisp of a thought
Goes flitting by.
Grasping, I whisk the empty air,
Wondering why.

Is it that I must seek,
Never to find,
The words that may express
My laboring mind?

Yet there are joys
To lighten my care;
The true pleasure lies
In one's courage to dare.

For the goal once attained,
And the spirit at rest,
We find our delight
Was all in the quest.

## AN OLD BOOK
### By GEOFFREY

Here, 'mid these faded pages may be found,
Not sheaves of chaff, but only ripened grain,
The wisdom of the Ages which has ta'en
The whole world's life to garner, food profound
For those whom prismic views of life astound;
For those who toil, though seemingly in vain;
For wisdom-hungry souls of men, who fain
Would know from whence they come, whither bound
Yet here it lies, a graybeard out of place,
All saddened that its lore is rarely scanned;
As Grecian temples, fated to outwear
Their purpose, 'mid the ruins of their race.
Irreverence and neglect on every hand,
Still lift their Doric shafts in silent prayer.

ALGERNON McSWAT                                                    *Sketches by Accident*

"I've Been Framed," Wailed the Diploma When It Found Itself Hung on the Wall.

### Prof's Mistake

'of. (exasperated): "Will
two fellows there in the back
the room quit exchanging
s?"

ude: "We ain't passin'
s. Them's dollar bills."

:of: "Dollar Bills?"

ude: "Yeh, we're shooting
s."

:of: "Oh, pardon me. I
ight you were passin' notes."

---

ie Applegate says he'd be
t up among the champs in
here game of golf if it were
for one fault. He stands too
: to the ball—after he hits it.

How will **I** explain this to **dad?** I don't
know whether **I'm** Osteopath or a
Knight of **Pythias.**

### Boy, Page Davey!

ummy—Why is the little fellow crying?
ummy—Because he can't have a holiday.
ummy—Why can't he have a holiday?
ummy—Because he doesn't go to school yet.

---

uestion—What has four legs and flies all around?
nswer—A dead horse.

Abie—Gif me apound of that
salmon.
Butcher—That isn't salmon.
That's ham.
Abie—Who asked you vat it
vas?—Jack o' Lantern.

### Adjusted Compensation

Grad—I've sure been a goat
these four years.
Junior—Well, that's why they
gave you a sheepskin.

### Plenty Big

Tom—"What was the biggest
thing you got in college?"
Sam—"My wife, she weighs
300 pounds."

---

Daughter—"Has my mail
come yet?"
Mother—"Daughter, you must
stop using that terrible slang."

---

First Room-mate: "That's a good tie you have on."
Second Ditto: "Yes, who gave it to you?"

---

Little girl (pointing to a toreador): "Ma, is that
one of those Spanish cuspidors?"

---

"Liza, le's you and me get mah'ied?"

"Boy, if youse jes' got to be crazy, whyn't you be
one of these here kleptomaniacs and make it pay?"

**A Dog's Life**

1st Childhood—Watcha goin' to do to that dog-house, mister?

2nd Childhood—I'm goin' to build in a closet so's the dog can hang up his pants.—Exchange.

---

Poet—"I am out here to get local color for a pastoral poem."

Farmer—"I reckon you're gettin' it, mister! I painted that settee only this mornin'."

---

"My sucker is broke," said the fair one as she asked the fountain boy for another straw. The sensitive escort would have sworn that she looked straight at him.—Mugwump.

---

IT'S BETTER TO BE BROKE THAN NEVER TO HAVE LOVED AT ALL.—Medley.

---

He had mastered the art of public speaking as taught at a modern university, and was giving his first public address after his graduation.

"The schoolwark is the housebull," he began, and stopped abashed at the tittering that followed his remarkable assertion.

"The schoolbull is the housewark—" he was groping blindly. He seized upon the water pitcher and drank deeply.

"The schoolhouse, my friends," triumphantly, "is the woolbark—"

He fainted and they carried him out.—Frivol.

---

Prof: "Can any one tell me what a stoic is?"

Abie (from the east side): "A stoic is a boid what brings little babies."

---

An educated man is one who can quote Shakespeare without crediting it to the Bible.

---

**Perfect**

"Give us an example of how circumstances alter cases."

"Milwaukee isn't famous any more."

---

Student (preparing for exams): "Gee, I wish someone would come in and argue me into going to a show."

---

"Have you been reading Longfellow?"

"Only about ten minutes."

---

He—I put a box on my window sill, filled it with dirt and planted seeds in it. What do you think came up?

Him—I'll bite. What did?

He—The cop. He told me to take it away.—Stone Mill.

---

A young lady was being interviewed.

"Do co-eds kiss?" she was asked.

"You'd be surprised," she remarked coyly, "how much goes on right under my nose."—Pelican.

---

THE DIFFERENCE BETWEEN A VIOLINIST AND A FIDDLER IS JUST ABOUT FOUR INCHES OF HAIR.—Widow.

---

Rastus—Dat sure am a flamin' tie you got on, Sambo.

Sambo—Yo sure am right, Rastus. Ah got it at a fire sale.—Ski-U-Mah.

---

We've always pitied the bachelor. He has no home to stay away from.—Lampoon.

---

Prof.: "Why are you taking this course, Mr. Brown?"

Stud: "Er, well, because I am very fond of the subject. It gives me a new insight into the problems which er—er—I am called upon to meet in every day life. It has been an inspiration to me."

Prof.: "Very good. Now, Mr. Smith, you tell one."

---

**A Little Pull**

Souse No. 1—"Les go shee 'The Covered Wagon.'"

Souse No. 2—"Can't. We're broke."

Souse No. 1—"Thash alright. I know the driver."—Juggler.

---

**Sonnut**

An aspiring young freshman, named Vance,
Attended the All-Students' dance;
　　The crowd gave a hoot
　　When they saw his dress-suit,
For the coat was not mate to the pants.

**In Love-Crazy**

"How do you know he's in love?"

"What else would make a man absent-minded enough to put his dirty shirt to bed and then jump down the clothes chute?"—Sun Dodger.

DARRELL DOWNS. 26

## TO SHINGLE OR NOT TO SHINGLE

To shingle or not to shingle—that is the question;
Whether 'tis better in the end to suffer
As one who stands against outrageous custom,
Or to take arms against a sea of troubles,
And with the shears to end them.  To curl the hair
No more; and with this shingle to say we end
The heart-ache and the thousand petty shocks
That pride is heir to; 'tis a consummation
Devoutly to be wished.  To be in style;
In style; the present style; aye, there's the rub;
For when this season's o'er what change may come,
When we have clipped our treasuerd golden locks,
Must give us pause: There's the respect
That makes calamity of changing style;
For who would wear the dress of ancient days?
The old remodeled hat, the last year's suit,
Who'd keep the shabby boots, the raw display
Of out-worn etiquette, who'd take the jibes
That those in style to the unstylish give,
He himself might e'en Beau Brummel be
Without a fear?  Who would old woolens wear
But that the dread of something after this—
The undiscovered style to whose advent
All women turn—puzzles the will
And makes us rather nurse the griefs we have
Than fly to others that we know not of.

A. A.

Jersey Judge: "So you murdered your family, eh?
Thirty days!"
Prisoner: "Don't be too hard on me, yer honor.  It
was only a small family."—Medley.

Night Watchman—"Young man, are you going to
kiss that girl?"
He (straightening up)—"No, sir."
Night Watchman—"Here, then; hold my lantern."

### Collegian Slouch

The other day
I went down to
A haberdashery
In quest of
A new hat.
I begged to be shown
The latest
Collegian models,
And having found one
To my liking
I asked the salesman
To give it the latest
Collegian block,
And so
Holding the hat
In one hand,
He raised the other
And brought it down
Forcefully
On the center of
The crown
And handed it
To me.
Salesmen have
A low sense of
Humor.

### Fish as a Brain Food

Thirty-six students at the University of Washington
are enrolled in the School of Fisheries, the only col-
lege of this kind in the United States.

Such an education presents benefits to be angled for,
when, after competing keenly for first plaice, each one
receives his sheepshead skin he will be able to face
the world unherringly without floundering or craw-
fishing, secure in his knowledge of the dark ways of
sharks and lobsters.  Whether he chooses to run with
the school or to strike out for himself with an entirely
different porpoise, he can always feel that the world
is his oyster.

It sounds like a whale of a course.

"Father, I think it's only fair to tell you I need fifty
dollars.  I'd rather owe it to you than some rank out-
sider."

Him—"I hear May was quite a fizzle in the play."
—"Yes, since she had her hair bobbed she misses her que."

---

### Habit Clings

The old-timer, who worked his way through college is now working his son's way through.

---

### Persistency

"Glad to see you at the dance, Chuck."
"Yeh, come near not bein' here."
"How's that?"
"I flipped to see whether I should come here or study Chem, and I had to do it six times before it came out right."

---

### Does

"We're off!" howled the chauffeur;
"He's skidding!" shrieked the maid.
"Fifty dollars," said the judge.
And the woman paid?
Not on your life she didn't.—Do Do.

Nanette: "Did you find Archie rather shy last night?"
Minnette: "A little. I had to pay our fares home."
--Pelican.

---

Nothing takes you off your feet like a comfortable chair.—Lampoon.

---

### Can't Even Throw a Thought

Bride: "I had a horrid dream. I dreamt that you were about to desert me."
Groom: "Holy smoke, I've married a mind-reader."
—Reel.

---

Issac—"Papa, what is a cynic?
Papa—"A sinick my poy—a sinick is the place where mama washes the dishes in.—Lampoon.

---

### BREAKFAST FUEL.

When breakfast foods are all the rage,
In this modern day and age,
A cautious person looks to see
Lest the dish before him be
     Excelsior.

The way they mix up corn and wheat,
We never know just what we eat.
The pure food laws seem all a myth,
When our poor jaws are tangled with
     Excelsior.

The choicest hay and straw solution
Will never help one's constitution.
So use these brands with names so fair
To start the morning fire, for they're
     Excelsior.

---

### Exempt From Income Tax

May—"What is your husband's average income?"
Fay—"Oh, about 2:00 a. m."

---

The only difference between a collegian and a $20 a week clerk, is that the $20 a week clerk wears the clothes for which the collegian is famous.

---

### Poetry?

There was an old lady from Lynn,
Who was so exceedingly thin
     That when she essayed
     To drink lemonade,
She slipped thru the straw and
     fell in.

---

Some of the wiser students are already at work on their "wonderful vacation" story. This will give them ample time to rehearse it before an audience of cows and chickens so that it will be free from inconsistencies next September.

---

### That's the Question

"It there an interesting story in connection with this arch?"
"Yes; but it's way over your head."
(Ed. Note. He meant the arch. See?)—Lampoon.

---

"Handy literal translations for all diplomas!"

## VACATION DETOUR

(Continued from Page 19)

whatever means we look out upon the universe, when we come to understand and see we find that this is a system of magnificent order. So also has the Creator writen laws upon your nature. You cannot break them and escape the penalty. Reckless abuse or misuse of the powers which are given you, lawless indulgence in pleasures, must result in the dethronement of your manhood. The only way into a princely manhood is that of self-control, self-denial, the temperate use of all things, ever subordinating the physical to the moral and spiritual. Take care of your body. Once break it down by neglect or by abuse of physical law, and you will be a lifelong loser by it. The body is the machinery; by it and through it alone can the mind it and the duties of life be fulfilled. Saysy H. W. Beecher, "There is an organization which we call the nervous system in the body, to which belong the functions of emotion, intelligence, sensation; and it is intimately connected with the whole circulation of the blood, with the condition of the blood as affected by the liver and by the aeration in the lungs. The manufacture of blood is dependent upon the stomach; so man is what he is, not in one part or another, but all over. One part is intimately connected with the other, from the animal stomach to the throbbing brain; and when a man thinks, he thinks the whole trunk through." These are physiological truths every man would know and carefully consider. I do not believe with some of our modern naturalists that man is simply a rertort into which certain things are cast and there chemically acted upon, producing as the case may be the fine play of thought, the sweet thrill of mother love or the brutal passion of a ravisher or murderer. This is a theory that certainly makes a "god of the belly." There are many ways in which men break the laws of health. One of the crying evils of our age is overwork. We live at high pressure. Men do not walk; they stride rapidly, and would run if dignity did not hold the check-rein. They do not breathe; they gasp. Like Rufus Choate they use up their constitution early, and then live on the by-laws. Intemperance is another great evil of health, as lack of rest is a great death blow to it.

HAVE a sane vacation. Go home and help your parents all you can; for this is their busy season. Remember they work nine months out of the year for you.. Get your feet below that table which is loaded with the good wholesome food that only your mother knows how to prepare. Get all the physical and mental rest you can. Go to bed early. At an opportune time during the summer give your HEART and SOUL

to a two or three-week pleasure jaunt. If you live in the vicinity of the mountains, spend some time in them, for they are refreshing. If in the Minnesota lake district, enjoy yourself there, for it is beautiful. If you are close to the Black Hills, travel through them, for they are wonderful. If you want to enjoy yourself, keep well by being hardy. Get your chance in this vacation at long tramps and hard beds and rough; be as clean, however, all through and all over as you are in the class-room, and then you will not only be able to come back to your school work in the fall, but you will come back and do your school work and enjoy it as much as you did your vacation.

## "IT MIGHT HAVE BEEN"

(Continued from Page 17)

day. Every time I am trying to think of some new twist in a design for a house, I seem to imagine the two of us living there, and I put my whole heart and soul into it, just as though I were planning it for you and me, and perhaps some day— children.

Ir—Now, Arthur, don't get sentimental. Don't you be thinking of serious things all the time. We are young and must have our fling. I believe in getting all the fun I can out of life.

Art—Perhaps you do, Irene; but deep down in your heart you know that you cannot get any real happiness out of this mad scramble for pleasure. But here, I'll have to quit this preaching. I almost forgot about supper. I'm as hungry as a bear.

Ir—Oh yes, I forgot. Ellen Hemingway called up today and invited us over to dinner this evening. You know they have just got settled in their new house on Longshore Drive.

Art—That's capital! I'll have to hurry up and get

ready. Is my dark suit back from the cleaner's?

Ir—Yes, Arthur, but I wish you would wear your tuxedo. You know you look well in it.

Art—Why, this isn't a dress affair, is it? We've known the Hemingways for years, and I'm sure George wouldn't wear a tuxedo at such an informal affair as this. Besides, I think my old "tux" needs pressing, I haven't worn it for such a long time.

Ir—Oh! I wanted to show Ellen that my husband was always well dressed, whatever the occasion. You know I'd give anything to have the opportunity to make her feel inferior.

Art—Now that's not a nice way to talk about friends; and as for the clothes, my dark suit is good enough. I'll go and change now.

Ir—Phone for a cab, will you?

Art—Why all this style? The street car is good enough. We should be economizing if we are ever going to have a house.

Ir—We will go in a taxi. I'll phone myself, to make sure.

The woman having the last word the curtain falls on

THE END OF ACT ONE.

ACT TWO

Scene—Living room of the Hemingway bungalow. There is a trace of newness in the room, but for all that it has a comfortable and homelike atmosphere. It is a little more spacious than the Morrison living room, and it expresses more individuality in its furnishings. George Hemingway and Irene Morrison enter from the left and seat themselves on the davenport. Ellen Hemingway and Arthur Morrison follow them in and take chairs, the four of them sitting in a friendly circle. George takes out cigarettes and offers one to Morrison. They smoke. He also offers one to Irene, but she refuses.

## NICE LITTLE PUPPY

(Continued from Page 14)

that what parts of the house had been left standing by the explosion must certainly be shaken down by her approach. Her arrival in the room pictured a burst of astonishment. She was postively inarticulate. She gazed around, bewildered, at the hill of plaster, lath and furniture.

"Wha—" She was just forming a word when she caught sight of a fold of Mr. Finkelstein's night shirt protruding from the heap.

"Papa! Isaac! HEL—UP!" She flung herself upon the pile and commenced frantically to extricate the elder Finkelstein. Tremendous were her exertions. Positively Amazonian were the pushings and pullings, the calls and entreaties, the imprecations and threats of dire vengeance which she gave vent to until she succeeded in pulling the limp form of her conjugal partner from the pile of debris. Once having done so, she snatched him up, as if he were a poorly-joined rag doll, and holding him to her allowed his dangling limbs to hang suspended and swaying from her ample bosom. She moved toward the sofa, the meantime crooning brokenly to him.

"Baby, my baby. Papa, what is it? Did you get hurt? Did something fall on you? Oh, my poor papa. There, there."

She placed him on the sofa and taking his hands in hers, stroked them tenderly, the while she promiscuously rained down resounding caresses upon his pale, upturned face. These proceedings had gone on for perhaps a few minutes when Mrs. Finkelstein thought she detected a slight sound behind her. On turning, she saw to her consternation that the wreckage at the far side of the room was moving. The whitened form of a man arose amidst the splintered laths. He stood for a moment, as if uncertain what to do, then rubbed the dust from out his eyes. Mrs. Finkelstein sat still and stared. She could think of absolutely nothing to say—or rather, in her horror, she could not think at all. As the man started to come forward she found her voice in the cry.

"Stay away! Don't come near! Stay back!"

Abie halted.

"Mama, don't you know? Its me, your Abie!"

"Oh! no. Could it be . . . . ? Oh, Abie, Abie!"

She ran forward and seized him in her arms, a place which, for once, he found quite satisfying. She looked at him.

"Are you here, too? Why, Abie, what is it? Your head? You got hurt!"

Abie put his hand to his head and brought it away slightly stained with blood. Immediately, he began to feel weaker. His mother half carried him to a chair, in which he limply dropped. With a hurried, "I-be-back-in-a-minute,'' Mrs. Finkelstein left the room for cloths and a basin. When she returned in a few moments, having slipped into a wrap, Abie personallly held out very little hope for his own recovery. But presently, with his head swathed in bandages, he began to feel better, and consequently more embarrassed However, his mother seemed to feel absolutely no curiosity with regard to the unusual circumstances. At any rate she expressed none. She was to intent upon the revival and comfort of her patients.

So far as she could see, her husband had escaped injury, save for a slight bruise on the head. She bathed his forehead in cold water. His breathing became more regular and some color returned to his cheeks. In direct proportion as these favorable signs appeared in his father, Abie's uneasiness increased. He would have liked to run away, but since no avenue of escape presented itself, he perforce decided to remain and take his medicine.

Mr. Finkelstein stirred and his eyes opened wearily. He did not at once comprehend the situation.

"What is it, Mamma?" He looked at her in wonder Then consciousness flooded back to him and he sat up as sternly as his weakness would permit. His eyes roved about the room until they settled upon Abie where they remained in silence for a moment. Abie slouched in his chair, ventured a hesitant glance at his father, then dropped his eyes to his hands, one of which he held tightly clasped within the other.. In growing apprehension, the mother glanced from father to son.

Finkelstein arose, swaying, to his feet, and pointing his finger at his son, said:

"So, it is you; you for whom I was so proud. You could do it. You—for whom I had so much ambitions. He paused a moment, while two great tears rolled down his cheeks. "Oh, Abie! For vy—— for vy did you do it?"

"Papa, Papa, what do you say to him?" But Abie said never a word; only crouched down a little further in his chair.

"Keep quiet, Mamma," said Finkelstein. "I vill the dealings. So you don't answer, hey? But I know So you could spend it with those loafer friends of you You are a bummer too. All you t'ink of is to spend 'nd spend, 'nd spend. You t'ink money is made for nothing but to throw out. Bah! You would make even a bummer of a Gentile. I t'ink I should throw you out with your bag and baggages.''

At the mention of the last faint threat, Abie fell his knees and held out his hands supplicatingly, while his mother ran to protect him, as if, for all the world the very life of her offspring were in danger.

Abie groaned dismally.

"No, no, Papa! You wouldn't? It was not on the

(Continued on Page 39)

### THE CREIGHTON DRAMATIC CLUB

(Continued from Page 11)

stricted organization impose limitations upon any dramatic society. With the present plan it is impossible to get a line on all the talent in the University. Many students who have genuine talent do not get an opportunity to show their worth because the Director cannot afford the experiment with unknown quantities. The success of a play is too important to risk a failure in any role. Yet it must be recognized that until some way can be found to discover and develop the new talent, the club cannot make such progress as it has a right to hope for with the material at hand. Moreover, those who are in close touch with dramatic activities at Creighton University, recognize that an enthusiastic and appreciative student audience will never be had until participation in University dramatics is made more wide and more general. They believe that the apparent lack of interest on the part of the student body is due to the fact that the great majority of the students have no contact whatever with dramatic work. Accordingly, they believe that the problem must be met by a policy which will insure more dramatics among a greater number of students.

What particular form this policy should take is a problem yet to be solved. A great many suggestions have been made. In the main, they contemplate the formation of small independent clubs, which may or may not be departmental in their membership. These clubs might organize for the purpose of producing one-act plays and short entertainments for special occasions. Their work would be entirely independent of that of any other organization, while at the same time they might count on co-operation of the general Director of dramatics and of the executive officers of the dramatic club. The responsibility, however, would rest entirely on the individual clubs. Some such plan as this seems the only possible way of getting the greatest number of students into dramatic work. The director of dramatics is more than sufficiently occupied with the activity of the Dramatic Club itself, whose membership is kept small and he, obviously, can be personally responsible for only a limited amount of work. But if the suggestion were carried out by certain groups of students, it would be a fairly easy matter to co-ordinate their activities for the general development of the dramatic art. Under this plan the energy would come from below, while the Dramatic Club, under its Director, would exert only a regulating influence.

Of course, it is apparent that such a plan is open to very grave criticism. Perhaps its greatest defect lies in the fact that it is ordinarily difficult to find persons who will take the initiative. But it is undoubtedly a

fact that there are men in the University who have enough interest in dramatic work to become the moving spirits in such organizations. If these men were to take up the work and receive a fair amount of cooperation, the success of the plan is not at all impossible.

The plan outlined here has been proposed in greater detail by various members of the Dramatic Club. What has been said will serve, however, to point out the main lines along which progress and expansion in dramatic activity at Creighton is likely to proceed. It is clear that there are problems confronting those who are interested in dramatics, and that some effort is being made to solve those problems. If it can be impressed upon a sufficient number of the students that these problems are worth solving, progress in dramatics will soon be made.

It is extremely important that the student body should be awakened to the necessity of forging ahead in dramatics. There is no reason why Creighton should not equal or surpass the standards set in other schools. We have the talent, we have the material equipment and we are peculiarly fortunate in having a very able Director. It is worth while getting behind dramatics.

## "IT MIGHT HAVE BEEN"

(Continued From Page 28)

Ir—I hate to go like this. Ellen, are you sure you don't mind?

Ell—Of course I don't. Go and have a good time.

Geo—(Rising) All right. Irene, get your wraps and come along. (They exit, right, talking).

Ir—(Coming in, right, with her hat and coat on) Good bye, folks.

Geo—(Who has followed her in) Good-bye; we'll be back by eleven or a little after.

Ellen and Arthur have risen and have followed them to the door. They all chorus good-bye. Ellen comes back and sits on the davenport. Arthur takes a chair.

Ell—If it were daylight I should ask you to look at my garden. You say you are interested in flowers.

Art—Let's not talk about gardens. Let us talk about ourselves.

Ell—Well, I'm afraid we cannot say anything new on the subject. I have known you all your life and guess I understand you as well as you do yourself.

Art—All women think they understand all men.

Ell—If you become brilliant, I'm afraid I can't hold up my end of the conversation.

Art—Seriously, Ellen, I believe we would get along much better in this world if we understood people and they really understood us. The trouble with people who become estranged is that they feel they haven't much in common.

ll—Yes, that's so. Here I have been married for a
year, and while I think I understand George al-
most perfectly, I have a feeling that he doesn't
understand me. We differ in our views on so
many things, and we are always trying to convince
each other that we are right.

rt—Well, at least that makes things interesting. It
would be pretty dull if you both thought the same
about everything.

ll—Yes, but George and I are of entirely different
temperaments. He wants lots of excitement. He
likes to dance and is always trying to get me to
go to parties. I like to stay at home and rest. A
quiet and peaceful life is my ideal.

rt—Yes, I know, but still we have to make the best of
things like that. I don't believe that there are any
two persons who agree on everything. Married
life is just one compromise after another. The
reason for so many failures in marriage is that peo-
ple fail to realize that they must bear and forbear.
The first year is usually the hardest.

ll—But you and Irene have been married for three
years, and still you disagree on almost everything.

rt—Yes, but we do not quarrel about everything.
When our tastes differ, she goes her way and I go
mine. I admit it is not an ideal arrangement, but
it is the best under the circumstances.

ll—But that makes you drift farther apart, and that
is almost as bad as quarreling.

rt—Whoever it was who said that marriages are made
in heaven didn't know what he was talking about.
They are not divinely prearranged; on the con-
trary, they are strictly earthly, and as in all other
mundane things there is room for mistakes.

ll—You seem to be somewhat of a cynic.

rt—No, not really a cynic in the accepted sense. We
are all cynics in a way, however, unless we have
never been disillusioned,—and there are few people
who have not had that experience. The best way is
to take things philosophically. And as for love,
that is not something magic which can be felt only
between two certain creatures. Love can be cul-
tivated. I think that a man can marry a woman
he doesn't really love, and in the course of years
can grow to love her.

ll—Do you believe in love at first sight?

rt—No; that is not real love. However, it may be a
preliminary. People cannot really love until they
know one another. This love at first sight is merely
admiration, or the attraction of one sex for the
other.

ll—I don't quite agree with you in all your views, but
I can see the reason for them. I think that certain
people were made for one another. When one
makes a mistake in marriage, his or her whole life
is marred.

Art—Well, they say a woman's heart is more often right than a man's head; but as to the truth or fallaciousness of that I won't give an opinion.

Ell—A woman has a head also.

Art—Yes, I'll admit that. Say, Ellen, do you still play the piano very often? I know before you were married you used to play divinely.

Ell—Flatterer. Just for that I'll make you the victim. (She goes to the piano. He turns the music for her. She plays, "Do You Remember?")

Art—That carries me back to my childhood. Do you remember, Ellen, when we used to play together?

Ell—Yes, Arthur, I don't believe I shall ever forget those days.

Art—And you know how we said that when we grew up we would marry and live happily ever after.

Ell—Yes, I know. It's funny how things turn out, isn't it? That childhood love was sacred to me.

Art—How did we drift apart? It seemed so gradual. Before I realized it I was married and settled down.

Ell—It's as you said. Our dreams rarely come true.

Art—If I had thought you really cared.

Ell—You know I did, Arthur.

Art—Who can help being cynical? I believe that it would have been better if I had married you, and George had married Irene.

Ell—You shouldn't say that.

Art—Why not say it? It's true, isn't it? One might as well say it as think it. Oh, Ellen, I know now that I have always loved you.

Ell—But Arthur, we are married now to others.

Art—Married. Yes, it's true. But why is it so? It is all wrong. I love you and you love me; you know you do.

(He takes her in his arms and kisses her. While they are still in each other's embrace the telephone rings. Ellen answers it).

Ell—Hello. Who?—Oh, George—What?—At the jail —Oh, Heavens! All right, I'll hurry—Good-bye (She hangs up the receiver). It's George. He said that the prohibition enforcement officers raided the roof garden and they have them at the jail. We'll have to go down and bail them out.

Curtains falls on the
END OF THE SECOND ACT.

### ACT THREE

Scene—Ante-room of the police court. Irene and George are seated on a bench in the corner of the room.

Geo—This is a fine mess we have gotten into.

Ir—We! You got me into it. You brought me there, I didn't know anything about the place. You should have had a little more consideration.

Geo—How did I know they were going to raid th

(Continued on Page 38)

## TWO VIEWS OF CONRAD

(Continued from Page 15)

is the handiwork of Conrad, it appears that we must ink the critical eye. The plot has the appearance of framework to support the superb patches of description, or of a canvas to receive deft strokes of characterization. But despite its rickety plot and sluggish action, the story has all the seductive charm of true romance, for it reeks of salt-water, love and adventure—a favorite blend with readers of romance.

CONRAD is perhaps without a peer as a stylist. He has a witchery of words that is positively uncanny, specially considering the fact that English is not his native tongue. From cover to cover, "The Rescue" reads as rhythmically as a piece of poetry. Conrad's language seems to ebb and flow as regularly as the tides which his descriptive pen so loves to linger over. He has succeeded in translating the unearthly rhythm of the sea and the waves into words. And with the accuracy of a faithful translator, he adapts sound and word to mood and action. One moment the sea is calm; aboard the brig, all is still; and Lingard's restless soul is relaxed; meanwhile the style is soft and subdued, in harmony with the peace that reigns around. But anon a squall strikes the ship, the decks of which become alive with pattering brown feet; Lingard's heart is wildly exultant, for he rejoices in this furious combat with the elements; and the language leaps and tumbles like the waves in their mad sport; it whispers like the wind and roars like the thunder; it has the same wild note of exultation as Lingard's ringing voice when it shouts orders to scurrying Malays. "The Rescue" is a superb study in style, and the very excellence of the style makes the defective plotting and the surplus of description all the more regrettable.

Anyone who picks up a Conrad romance cannot help being struck with the profusion of description. Conrad's descriptions are as lovely and luxurious as Lafcadio Hearn's, and as vivid as Stevenson's. The writer is adept in the use of atmospheric devices, and knows all the secrets of setting. He has the priceless gift of hitting off a whole situation or of flashing a whole scene on the mind's eye with a single startling epithet. I have read many a description of storms at sea, but none quite so vivid and striking as the one in the first book of "The Rescue." But beautiful as it is, this description bares one of Conrad's worst weaknesses; for it does not advance the plot an inch. The only excuse for its presence is the sheer beauty of it, and its mystic symbolism.

Recognizing and applauding Conrad's power in this respect, I still claim that he is too prodigal in the display of his descriptive gifts. Although my views with regard to description have altered essentially, I still

cling to my early contention that Conrad is excessively addicted to description. I do not mean that individual descriptions are long or tedious, but that descriptions recur too frequently. Conrad seems to know the value of brevity, but not of restraint. Description is rich fare for novel-readers, anyway, and must be doled out with niggardly hand. But Conrad's novels are an orgy of description; so much so that the appetite becomes cloyed with its rich diet, and the imagination becomes surfeited with setting. Accordingly, I am not ashamed of my first verdict on Conrad, since it is not without some foundation in fact and in the laws of good taste I like mince pie as well as the next fellow; but half a dozen hellpings is a little too much even for me. I don't propose to get mental dyspepsia by indulging in food that is too rich for the mind.

---

### ENFORCEMENT IN LITTLE RIVER

(Continued From Page 8)

annoyance by a good deal of wild shooting, but as soon as they found that the new sheriff was in earnest they did not waste expensive ammunition. Nowadays the westerner is a harmless, though boisterous, fellow, who shoots but for noise, save when called upon to end the misery of a crippled steer.

"Boss" lost no time in taking advantage of favorable conditions. He watched "Tex" with one eye and business with the other. Any liquor that went to relieve the freshly accentuated thirst of the county passed through his hands, netting a substantial profit. But no good lacks an admixture of evil. After "Tex" had quieted things at Cimmarron and Idabel, he began to spend more time at Cactus Bend. This seriously interfered with trade, and, wh at further alarmed "Boss," seemed to take Peggy's mind off her work.

The week before election "Boss" persuaded "Tex" to withdraw as a candidate for sheriff, and promised to put him in charge of the Double Bar as soon as his present term expired.

The morning the polls opened "Tex" was authoritatively informed of a deplorably lawless spot somewhere out in the county. He rode forth to his duty.

Business flourished at the Dusty Burro. Not only could few recall a more exciting election, but none could remember a wetter occasion. One thing disturbed the serenity of the occasion for "Boss." I was rumored that many were writing in "Tex's" name on the ballots.

By evening things had quieted, chiefly because the available supply of pink lightning had given out. Riders and flivvers came into the Bend from polls in the county, with the news that "Tex" was almost surely elected.

Peggy was staying late at the Dusty Burro. The flickering oil lamps were already shedding their yellow smoky light. A man near the bar inoffensively raised a half empty pint bottle to his lips.

"I wish you would not drink in here," protested Peggy.

The front screen door opened and "Tex" came in hesitatingly. The poor fellow with the flask looked round at first in surprise and then in terror. The bottle fell from his hands, and was smashed on the floor.

"Tex" laughed. "Well, the evidence is gone, anyway. Have you any more of it on you?"

The addressed made a hasty exit.

"Tex" turned toward Peggy, who was coming round to sweep up the glass. "You didn't sell him that, did you?" he questioned.

"You know I wouldn't, 'Tex,' don't you?" she answered.

"Of course I—ought to."

He was about to take the broom from her to sweep up the glass, when some revelation from the depths of her eyes prompted him to take her from the broom.

Just at this juncture "Boss" rode down the street to the door of the hotel, rather disgruntled. He dismounted, but on seeing the pair standing a little too close together to warrant intrusion, he backed away. He stood with an elbow resting on a hitching post and the corresponding hand propped under his chin. "Boss" began to think—

"Tex" had made good all around—"Boss" was glad of that—It was a little hard to lose Peggy—but youth must be served—"Tex" would be sheriff two years more—maybe "Tex" and Peggy could make a go of the Dusty Burro—sure they could—He himself would devote his time to the Double Bar—a good ranch needed lots of attention—Bootlegging was no profession for a gentleman, anyway.

"Boss" tossed the loose rein over the pony's neck, and rode resignedly away.

---

### SONGS IN A SHOWER ROOM
(Continued from Page 9)

in the spirit of the young romantic lover addressing his sweetheart as "My Sunshine." It is not fair to interpret in the same meaning to the outburst of the tired two-miler in the shower-room. I have heard football teams express the joy of victory in the triumphant strains of "A Sole Mio." I have heard these same teams drown the sorrow of defeat in the identical strains, though this time, in a minor key. "O Sole Mio" is by all means the best shower-room song that has ever been written.

If any one still holds to the tradition of wine as the inspiration of song, let him follow the example of our poet. If he has a song in his heart, if he would know the joy of an exuberant spirit, free and unrestrained, why, then, let him bathe often.

### "IT MIGHT HAVE BEEN"

(Continued from Page 34)

place?

Ir—You seemed to know well enough when the police came. You tried to duck out and leave me there alone.

Geo—I did not. And then instead of keeping still and letting me do the talking, you had to spill the whole thing by telling them our names.

Ir—I thought when they knew who we were they would let us go.

Geo—Yes, this is a fine fix. Think of it in the papers tomorrow: "George Hemingway arrested with another man's wife." That will make fine reading, won't it?

Ir—Well, do you suppose I like it? Most likely they will have my name in bigger print than yours. Oh, I wish I hadn't gone out with you.

Geo—That wish is mutual. I thought you were a good sport. I don't like it any more than you do. From the way you talk one would think that I had it all arranged for my own special pleasure.

Ir—Oh, I wish Arthur would come. I want to get out of this place.

Geo—I am not enjoying it very much, myself.

Ir—Oh, if Arthur were here, he would at least be sympathetic. You act as if it were all my fault.

Geo—And you are trying to lay the blame for the whole thing on me.

(The door is opened and a policeman appears. "Here they are, right in here". He ushers in Ellen and Arthur and going out closes the door.)

Art—You are a good one, you are. It isn't enough that you leave your wife at home while you run wild, but you have to drag my wife into it. If you didn't neglect your own wife so much, and thought a little of her feelings, you wouldn't have to find amusement by running around with other men's wives. You're a fine one.

Ell—Why, Arthur! What do you mean talking to my husband that way? George isn't any more to blame than Irene. He just wanted to show her a good time, something which she did'nt get from you. And as for neglecting me, I guess I am not any more neglected than Irene.

Art—Why, Ellen! What makes you talk that way? You're all unstrung because of this.

Ell—No, I am just seeing things in the right light for the first time. I know I have been rather foolish, but I know what I am talking about now.

Ir—Don't blame Arthur, Ellen; it's all my fault. He hasn't neglected me; it is I who have neglected him.

Art—I had it fixed up so there will be nothing about this in the papers; so you needn't worry.

Geo—Well, let's get out of here, Ellen.

E—Perhaps I spoke a little hastily, but at any rate let us be friends. I think I have really learned something to-night. Take me home, George.

G—Yes. I guess that's where we belong. I think I shall appreciate home a little more after this. (They go out).

I—Well, Arthur, I don't suppose that you can forgive me. I really deserve this, I have been so selfish.

At—Nonsense, Irene. Ellen told the truth; I have been neglecting you and thinking only of myself, and this is only the natural outcome. You are young and want pleasure, and I have been blind not to see it.

I—No, Arthur; all I want is to have you take me back home. I have been mean in running off and leaving you alone. I hate to say it, but I know I ought, for I have been flirting with George and trying to get him to make love to me. Maybe you despise me for it. I know it is hard for you to forgive me, but I really am sorry.

At—Why, of course I forgive you. We all are a little foolish at some time or another.

I—Oh, Arthur! (They embrace and kiss).

I—Arthur, tomorrow I want you to take my two thousand dollars out of the bank and get that home in Forest Lawn. It's time we settled down.

The curtain falls.

THE END OF THE PLAYLET.

## NICE LITTLE PUPPY

(Continued from Page 30)

was going to spend it. It was—a—it was for business, papa, yes, Papa,—truly, it was for business. I could make it, in a short time, into twice as much." He looked questioniugly at his father. "Maybe three times as much."

The parental ire subsided somewhat.

"Oh, you don't say so. For vy you didn't come at once to me, then?"

Mama Finkelstein, who had brightened considerably at the previous revelation, was again crest-fallen. Suddenly she smiled.

"Oh, I know. It was for a surprise. It was for a surprise on papa, wasn't it Abie, darling?"

He looked at her rather dumbly and nodded.

"You see, papa, it was for a surprise. Abie wished for to surprise you when he brought the money in." She looked at her husband, her eyes large with hope.

"Oh, vel . . . . . ."

A rather imperious knock was heard at the door. Mr. Finkelstein rushed out for a wrapper, and his wife went to the door.

"Say, does a dago by the name of Abie Finkelstein stay here?" It was an unpleasantly shrill feminine voice. At sound of it Abie positively shrunk.

"Yes, no, but yes, but you couldn't ....."

"Out of my way, lady. Who said I couldn't?" Th young woman bounded into the room just as Mr. Finke stein returned. She suffered him a momentary glance and then turning to Abie, who was trying to articula something, she shot at him a rapid-fire questionaire.

"So this is where you stuck, is it? Thought you leave me waiting all day for you at the church, did you I guess not. I guess little old Lollie LaRue is a bit to wise for you. Say, dumb-bell, are you wise to the fa that our train leaves in a little over an hour, and we' not married yet? Take it from me, kid, and move."

She paused. No one else uttered a sound. The tw Finkelsteins, father and mother, stood gazing at he with steely-eyed horror. Abie trembled. At length M Finkelstein, ignoring Miss Lollie, advanced to face h son.

"So!" It was like the bursting of a rubber balloo So! I was right then! This," pointing to Lolli "this is the reason why you would rob me. For this yo would rob your father, to marry out of the race. Bum mer! You is nothing but a bummer! You—, you—, The old man inarticulate. He stood for a moment, h hands clenched and his face purpling. Then, his eye flaring with anger, he shouted. "Git out and don come back!"

Now Lollie LaRue was wise in worldly wisdom. Th condition of the room told her part of the story, and in stinct pieced out the rest, so that she had a fairly clea idea of the situation. She had no intention of allowin so valuable a catch as Abie to get away from her, so tha when Mr. Finkelstein stepped back from his son, sh approached him.

At first, the evident repulsion with which he receive her advances kept her at arm's length; but, by dint o coaxing and cajoling, wheedling and argument, sh finally gained a hearing. The father listened sternl and impassively at first, then his features relaxed, the a broad smile covered his face, at which time he turne abruptly from the young woman and spoke to his so

"Abie, you old sneaker! Why you didn't tell you papa that her name wasn't really Lollie LaRue, bu Isabel Levinsky, and that she has a rich uncle, who sh is expecting maybe will die soo? Oh, you shouldn fool your papa that way." Abie was in a daze.

Mamma calls out, "The policers, Papa!"

Papa replies, "Police? Who told the police to com here? Tell them they should get out and not bothe me." Then turning to his son, he said, "Take her m boy."

And he did. And they lived happily for the first yea